The Cowls are not what they seem

SHANNON OKEY

The Cowls Are Not What They Seem

ISBN 13 (print): 978-1-937513-73-3
First Edition
Published by Cooperative Press
http://www.cooperativepress.com

Patterns © 2018 Shannon Okey
Photos © 2018 Shannon Okey
Models: Jennie Doran, Emily Williams, Larissa Brown

Every effort has been made to ensure that all the information in this book is accurate at the time of publication; however, Cooperative Press neither endorses nor guarantees the content of external links referenced in this book.

If you have questions or comments about this book, or need information about licensing, custom editions, special sales, or academic/corporate purchases, please contact Cooperative Press: info@cooperativepress.com or 10252 Berea Rd, Cleveland OH 44102 USA

No part of this book may be reproduced in any form, except brief excerpts for the purpose of review, without prior written permission of the publisher. Thank you for respecting our copyright.

For Cooperative Press
Senior Editor: Shannon Okey
Technical Editor: Andi Smith
Book Designer: Kayt de Fever

For Sherilyn Fenn. Because eyebrows.

And for Lisa Grossman, because love.

Introduction   8   Audrey   11   Diane   15

Log Lady   19   Donna   23   Grey-dient   27

Harriet   31   Josie   35

Laura 39

Nadine 41

Lucy 45

Norma 49

Maddie 53

Ronette 57

Shelly 61

Master Key 64

Introduction

This book started out as an experiment designed to support our yarnie friends who vend at Maryland Sheep and Wool each year. Could I design a cowl in each dyer's yarn (to be displayed in their booth, along with the pattern) to help them sell more? Could we do some kind of scavenger hunt to make sure festival guests got around to each individual booth? Well, yes. But only with a massive amount of help from both my longtime technical editor Andi Smith and dedicated sample knitters, most of whom are designers themselves (Karma Kauffman, Lars Rains, Erica Hernandez, Christina Bowers, Lisa Roman, Marie Duquette), did this project come to fruition.

We got all but one cowl done in time, and the one that didn't get finished (Ronette, at right, modeled by Cooperative Press author Larissa Brown) was done in Lisa Grossman's, aka Tsock Tsarina's yarn. Lisa passed away during the course of this project. The festival just hasn't the same for me without Lisa, and so I've dedicated this book to her.

Now, why the Twin Peaks sub-theme and punny title? I've been a longtime fan of the show, and used a rewatch for background noise during the design process, but then my brain started working. What's a cowl if not a tube, right? And I knit almost EVERYTHING in the round. Everything. I'll knit something in the round and steek it open before I'll knit it flat. It's my thing, what can I say? One of my book goals was to show you just how versatile tubular knitting can be. A sock is more or less a 64-st tube, with variations. A top-down raglan sweater is a tube once you're past the armpit area. So Andi and I cooked up a chart of stitch counts for each pattern and a very basic raglan sweater pattern you can use to convert the cowl of your choice to a sweater. (Fast forward to page 66 for that).

You can take this concept and apply it anywhere. Leg warmers! Wristlets. Whatever. So long as you've got an appropriate stitch count, and you're knitting in the round, it should be a snap to adapt. The cowls are not what they seem, indeed. (Note for non-Twin Peaks fans, "the owls are not what they seem" is a line from the show that people have debated for the past two decades. What it means exactly is still up in the air, if you ask me, even after watching Twin Peaks: The Return!)

Shannon Okey is a designer and also the publisher at Cooperative Press. She bases pretty much all her makeup choices on the character Audrey in Twin Peaks. No, really.

Audrey

Into The Whirled is our neighbor at Rhinebeck each year. I love their saturated colors like Atomic.

This stitch pattern resembles ocean waves to me, and would also be great in a blue or sea-green color. It just so happened that we shot these photos when Jennie (the model's) store was decorated for Valentine's Day in the front window, though!

Audrey

MATERIALS

Into The Whirled Fiber Arts Wyndham Worsted [100% Superwash Merino; 216 yds / 197.51m per 3.5 oz / 100g skein]; color: Atomic

1 32" US#9 / 5.5mm circular needle

1 US#10 / 6mm for cast on/bind off

Large-eyed, blunt needle for weaving in ends

Stitch marker

MEASUREMENTS

Circumference:
22" (before blocking)
23" (after blocking)

Height:
9.5" (before blocking)
10" (after blocking)

GAUGE

Large: width: 250 cm [98"], height: 128 cm [50"]

Small: width: 180 cm [71"], height: 97 cm [38"]

STITCH PATTERN

Rnd 1: Yo, ssk, [p1, k1tbl] 5 times; repeat to end of rnd

Rnd 2: Yo, p1, ssk, [k1tbl, p1] 4 times, k1tbl; repeat to end of rnd

Rnd 3: Yo, p2, ssk, [p1, k1tbl] 4 times; repeat to end of rnd

Rnd 4: Yo, p3, ssk, [k1tbl, p1] 3 times, k1tbl; repeat to end of rnd

Rnd 5: Yo, p4, ssk, [p1, k1tbl] 3 times; repeat to end of rnd

Rnd 6: Yo, p5, ssk, [k1tbl, p1] twice, k1tbl; repeat to end of rnd

Rnd 7: Yo, p6, ssk, [p1, k1tbl] twice; repeat to end of rnd

Rnd 8: Yo, p7, ssk, k1tbl, p1, k1tbl; repeat to end of rnd

Rnd 9: Yo, p8, ssk, p1, k1tbl; repeat to end of rnd

Rnd 10: Yo, p9, ssk, k1tbl; repeat to end of rnd

Rnd 11: Yo, p10, ssk; repeat to end of rnd

Rnd 12: Ssk, [p1, k1tbl] 5 times, yo; repeat to end of rnd

Rnd 13: Ssk, [p1, k1tbl] 4 times, p1, yo, p1; repeat to end of rnd

Rnd 14: Ssk, [p1, k1tbl] 4 times, yo, p2; repeat to end of rnd

Rnd 15: Ssk, [p1, k1tbl] 3 times, p1, yo, p3; repeat to end of rnd

Rnd 16: Ssk, [p1, k1tbl] 3 times, yo, p4; repeat to end of rnd

Rnd 17: Ssk, [p1, k1tbl] twice, p1, yo, p5; repeat to end of rnd

Rnd 18: Ssk, [p1, k1tbl] twice, yo, p6; repeat to end of rnd

Rnd 19: Ssk, p1, k1tbl, p1, yo, p7; repeat to end of rnd

Rnd 20: Ssk, p1, k1tbl, yo, p8; repeat to end of rnd

Rnd 21: Ssk, p1, yo, p9; repeat to end of rnd

Rnd 22: Ssk, yo, p10; repeat to end of rnd

Rnd 23: As rnd 1

FINISHING INSTRUCTIONS

Cast on 120 sts, with larger needle. Being careful not to twist, join to work in the round, adding a stitch marker to denote beginning of rnd.

Following either the chart or the stitch pattern, work rnds 1 - 23 once, rnds 2 - 23 once, and rnds 2 - 11 once. Bind off with larger needles.

Weave in ends and block.

Audrey

- ☐ Knit
- • Purl
- ꭆ Ktbl
- ○ Yarn over
- ╲ Ssk

Diane

I went through my stash in meticulous detail recently and it's almost embarrassing how often this particular color makes an appearance. Here, it serves as the perfect background for a series of intricate stitches.

The Verdant Gryphon's saturated version of my favorite absinthe-colored goodness also reminds me that the character it's named for (Agent Cooper's faceless assistant) probably needs a large drink on a regular basis given all she's got to deal with from his work.

Diane

MATERIALS

The Verdant Gryphon Bugga! [70% superwash Merino wool/ 20% Mongolian cashmere/ 10% nylon;

412 yds / 376.73m per 4.3 oz / 121g skein]; color: Paradise Valley;

1 32" US#5 / 3.75mm circular needle

Large-eyed, blunt needle for weaving in ends

2 stitch markers

MEASUREMENTS

Circumference:
26" (before blocking)
28" (after blocking)

Height:
10" at lowpoint, 12" at highpoint (before and after blocking)

GAUGE

2 sts x 28 rnds = 4" square in stitch pattern A, before blocking

STITCH PATTERN

Warning to knitter: It can be easy to get lost in the pattern since some rnds are similar. Be sure to leave yourself a note as to where you are in the pattern when you stop knitting. It would also be helpful to make it clear to yourself exactly which row you are currently knitting on by using sticky notes or a chart minder. The pattern itself is not that difficult.

Cast on 150 sts, join in the round, and place stitch marker at the beginning and after the 30th stitch.

Rnd 1: K1, p1; repeat to end of rnd

Rnd 2: P1, k1; repeat to end of rnd

Rnd 3: As rnd 1

Rnd 4: Work rnd 1 of chart A over first 30 sts, and work chart B over remaining sts.

FINISHING INSTRUCTIONS

Continue in pattern as set, for 94 rnds (two repeats of chart A) then work rnds 1 - 3 once more. Bind off.

Weave in ends and block.

Diane

(gray)	No stitch
(blank)	Knit
•	Purl
O	Yarn over
Ʀ	Ktbl
V	K, p, k into st
/	K2tog
\	Ssk
⑦	Sl4, k3tog, p4sso
⒜	K3tog
⒝	K4tog
⋏	Sl 1, k2tog, psso
⋏	Sl 1, k3tog, psso
⋏	Sl 2, k1, p2sso
⧅	1/1 LT
⧄	1/1 RT

Chart B

Diane

Chart B

Log Lady

I love Buffalo Gold. Ron and Theresa, the owners, have done so much to promote bison fiber in this country. They're constantly on the road doing shows and so much more.

What better color to pay tribute to the Log Lady than a natural one? The stitch pattern also reminds me of log bark.

Log Lady

MATERIALS

The Buffalo Wool Co. Tracks - Bison/Merino Sock Weight [90% Superwash Merino, and 10% Bison down; 400 yds / 366m per 4 oz / 113g skein]; color: Natural

1 32" US#4 / 3.5mm circular needle

Cable needle (optional)

Large-eyed, blunt needle for weaving in ends

Stitch marker

MEASUREMENTS

Circumference:
26" (before blocking)
28" (after blocking)

Height:
10" (before blocking)
12" (after blocking)

GAUGE

26 sts x 36 rnds = 4" square in stitch pattern before blocking

STITCHES USED

2/2 RC - slip 2 sts to cable needle, hold in back, k2, k2 from cable needle

2/2 LC - slip 2 sts to cable needle, hold in front, k2, k2 from cable needle.

STITCH PATTERN

Rnds 1 - 3: Knit

Rnd 4: 2/2 LC, k4, 2/2 RC; repeat to end of rnd

Rnds 5 - 7: Knit

Rnd 8: K2, 2/2 RC, 2/2 LC, k2; repeat to end of rnd

FINISHING INSTRUCTIONS

Cast on 168 sts, join to work in the round, adding a stitch marker to denote the beginning of the round.

Work repeats of the chart, or the stitch pattern for 10" and bind off.

Weave in ends and block to 28" x 12".

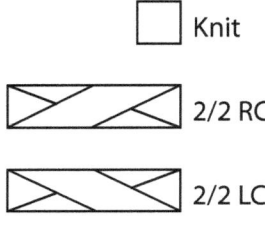
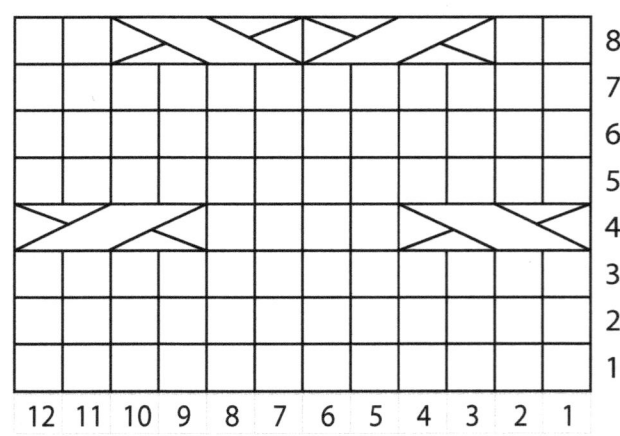

Donna

This green almost stole my heart away from chartreuse for a minute thanks to its depth. Like a forest full of pine trees it makes you stop and look twice (or more) at all the rich shades it contains.

Donna, the character it's named for, doesn't get nearly enough credit if you ask me. She's a tough cookie. The heavy texture of this cowl would make a spectacular sweater if you choose to adapt it.

Donna

MATERIALS

Spirit Trail Tayet [100% superwash Bluefaced Leicester wool, 325 yds / 297m per 4 oz / 113g skein];

1 32" US#7 / 4.5 mm circular needle

Large-eyed, blunt needle for weaving in ends

Stitch marker

MEASUREMENTS

Circumference:
24" (before blocking)
27" (after blocking)

Height:
9" (before and after blocking)

GAUGE

16 sts x 20 rnds = 4" square in stitch pattern before blocking

STITCH PATTERN

Rnd 1: P1, k2, yo, ssk, p1, ssk, k8, yo, k1, yo; repeat to end of rnd

Rnd 2 (and all even rnds): P1, k2tog, yo, k2, p1, ssk, k10; repeat to end of rnd

Rnd 3: P1, k2, yo, ssk, p1, ssk, k7, yo, k1, yo, k1; repeat to end of rnd

Rnd 5: P1, k2, yo, ssk, kp1, ssk, k6, yo, k1, yo, k2; repeat to end of rnd

Rnd 7: P1, k2, yo, ssk, p1, ssk, k5, yo, k1, yo, k3; repeat to end of rnd

Rnd 9: P1, k2, yo, ssk, p1, ssk, k4, yo, k1, yo, k4; repeat to end of rnd

Rnd 10: As rnd 2

FINISHING INSTRUCTIONS

Cast on 126 sts, and join to work in the round.

Rnd 1: Purl

Rnd 2: Knit

Rnd 3: Purl

Rnd 4: Knit

Rnd 5: Work repeats of the chart or stitch pattern words until the cowl is about 8.5" high.

Last 4 rnds:

1: Knit

2: Purl

3: Knit

4: Purl

Bind off.

Weave in ends and block.

Donna

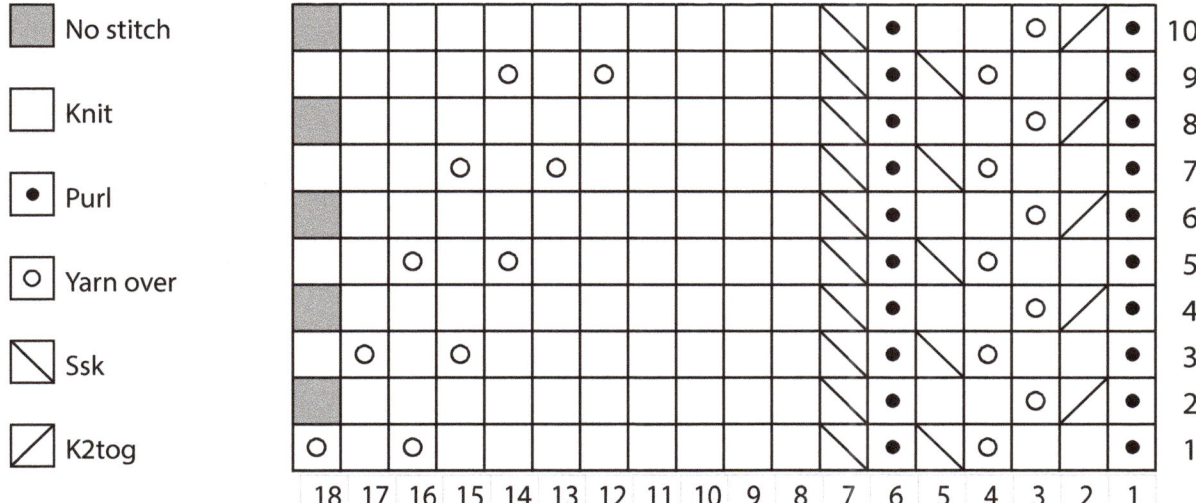

	No stitch
	Knit
•	Purl
○	Yarn over
╲	Ssk
╱	K2tog

Grey-dient

I like dye, but I am not a production dyer by a long shot. And though this one is knit from yarn I dyed myself, there are many possible gray, charcoal and dark gradients out there.

This is the color of the fog that rolls in over the mill in Twin Peaks, or the mist on the waterfall near the Great Northern hotel. Grey doesn't get as much love as bright colors but it's infinitely more versatile. Greys are a great counterpoint to strong and bright colors in your existing wardrobe.

Grey-dient

MATERIALS

Wool2Dye4 Quarter Round[100% Superwash Merino, 438 yds / 401m per 3.53 oz / 100g skein]; color: custom dyed, check Dragonfly Fibers Winter Woods or Miss Babs Ansel for similar grey tones;

1 32" US#4 / 3.5mm circular needle

Large-eyed, blunt needle for weaving in ends

Stitch marker

MEASUREMENTS

Circumference:
28" (before blocking)

Height:
9" (before and after blocking)

Note: these may vary if you use a different yarn!

GAUGE

24 sts x 24 rnds = 4" square in stitch pattern before blocking

STITCH PATTERN

Rnd 1: P1, yo, k1, p2, k2, k2tog, p2, ssk, k2, p2, k1, yo, p1; repeat to end of rnd

Rnd 2 (and all even rnds): Work the sts as they appear

Rnd 3: P1, k1, yo, k1, p2, k1, k2tog, p2, ssk, k1, p2, k1, yo, k1, p1; repeat to end of rnd

Rnd 5: P1, k2, yo, k1, p2, k2tog, p2, ssk, p2, k1, yo, k2, p1; repeat to end of rnd

Rnd 7: P1, k3, yo, k1, p1, k2tog, p2, ssk, p1, k1, yo, k3, p1; repeat to end of rnd

Rnd 9: P1, k4, yo, k1, k2tog, p2, ssk, k1, yo, k4, p1; repeat to end of rnd

Rnd 11: P1, 2/2 LC, p1, yo, k2tog, p2, ssk, yo, p1, 2/2 RC, p1; repeat to end of rnd

Rnd 13: P1, k4, p2, k1, p2, k1, p1, k4, p1; repeat to end of rnd

Rnd 15: P1, 2/2 LC, p2, k1, p2, k1, p2, 2/2 RC, p1, repeat to end of rnd

Rnd 17: P1, ssk, k2, p2, k1, yo, p2, yo, k1, p2, k2, k2tog, p1; repeat to end of rnd

Rnd 19: P1, ssk, k1, p2, k1, yo, k1, p2, k1, yo, k1, p2, k1, k2tog, p1; repeat to end of rnd

Rnd 21: P1, ssk, p2, k1, yo, k2, p2, k2, yo, k1, p2, k2tog, p1; repeat to end of rnd

Rnd 23: P1, ssk, p1, k1, yo, k3, p2, k3, yo, k1, p1, k2tog, p1; repeat to end of rnd

Rnd 25: P1, ssk, k1, yo, k4, p2, k4, yo, k1, k2tog, p1; repeat to end of rnd

Rnd 27: P1, ssk, yo, p1, 2/2 RC, p2, 2/2 LC, p1, yo, k2tog, p1; repeat to end of rnd

Rnd 29: P1, k1, p2, k4, p2, k4, p2, k1, p1; repeat to end of rnd

Rnd 31: P1, k1, p2, 2/2 RC, p2, 2/2 LC, p2, k1, p1; repeat to end of rnd

FINISHING INSTRUCTIONS

Cast on 180 sts, join to work in the round, adding a stitch marker to denote beginning of round.

Work repeats of the chart or stitch pattern until the cowl measures about 8 or 9" tall.

Bind off.

Weave in ends and block.

Grey-dient

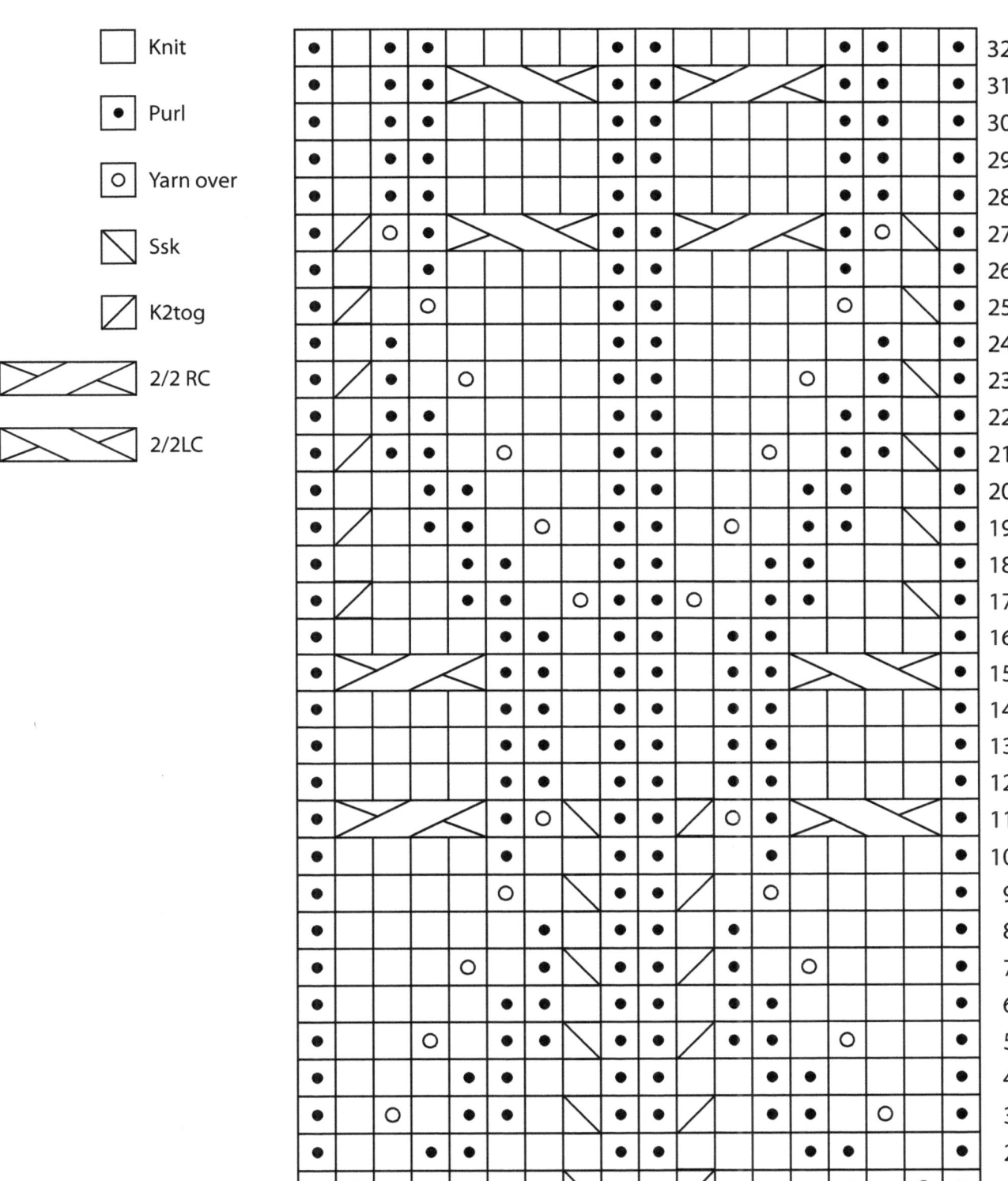

Harriet

I told you I liked green, ok?

Jill Draper does, too. I admit I have more than one of her green yarns in my personal stash, though it's her multicolors that usually catch my eye at shows. This simple cable cowl is elegant and looks good on everyone.

Harriet

MATERIALS

Jill Draper Mohonk [100% NYS Cormo Wool; 370 yds / 338 m per 4 oz / 113g skein]; color: Leaf;

1 32" US#8 / 5mm circular needle

Cable needle

Large-eyed, blunt needle for weaving in ends

Stitch marker

MEASUREMENTS

Circumference:
24" (before and after blocking)

Height:
7" (before and after blocking)

GAUGE

20 sts x 28 rnds = 4" square in stitch pattern before blocking

STITCHES USED

1/1 RT - slip 1 st to cable needle, hold in back, k1, k1 from cable needle

1/1 LT - slip 1 st to cable needle, hold in front, k1, k1 from cable needle

1/1 RTp - slip 1 st to cable needle, hold in back, k1, p1 from cable needle

1/1 LTp - slip 1 st to cable needle, hold in front, p1, k1 from cable needle

STITCH PATTERN

Rnd 1: P1, k2, p6, k2, p1; repeat to end of rnd

Rnd 2: P1, 1/1 RT, p6, 1/1 RT, p1; repeat to end of rnd

Rnd 3 (and all odd rnds): Work sts as they appear

Rnd 4: 1/1 RTp, 1/1 LTp, p4, 1/1 RTp, 1/1 LTp; repeat to end of rnd

Rnd 6: (See note above) P2, 1/1 LTp, p2, 1/1 RTp, p2, 1/1 LT; repeat to end of rnd

Rnd 8: 1/1 LTp, p2, 1/1 LTp, 1/1 RTp, p2, 1/1 RTp; repeat to end of rnd

Rnd 10: P1, k1, p3, 1/1 RT, p3, k1, p1; repeat to end of rnd

Rnd 12: 1/1 RTp, p2, 1/1 RTp, 1/1 LTp, p2, 1/1 LTp; repeat to end of rnd

Rnd 14: (See note above) P3, k1, p2, k1, p3, 1/1 LT; repeat to end of rnd

Rnd 16: 1/1 LTp, p2, 1/1 LTp, 1/1 RTp, p2, 1/1 RTp; repeat to end of rnd

Rnd 18: P1, k1, p3, 1/1 RT, p3, k1, p1; repeat to end of rnd

Rnd 20: 1/1 RTp, p2, 1/1 RTp, 1/1 LTp, p2, 1/1 LTp; repeat to end of rnd

Rnd 22: (See note above) P2, 1/1 RTp, p2, 1/1 LTp, p2, 1/1 LT; repeat to end of rnd

Rnd 24: 1/1 LTp, 1/1 RTp, p4, 1/1 LTp, 1/1 RTp; repeat to end of rnd

FINISHING INSTRUCTIONS

Cast on 120 sts, join in the round, adding a stitch marker to denote the beginning of the round.

Work 48 rnds of stitch pattern or chart, then bind off in pattern of rnd 1.

Weave in ends and block.

Harriet

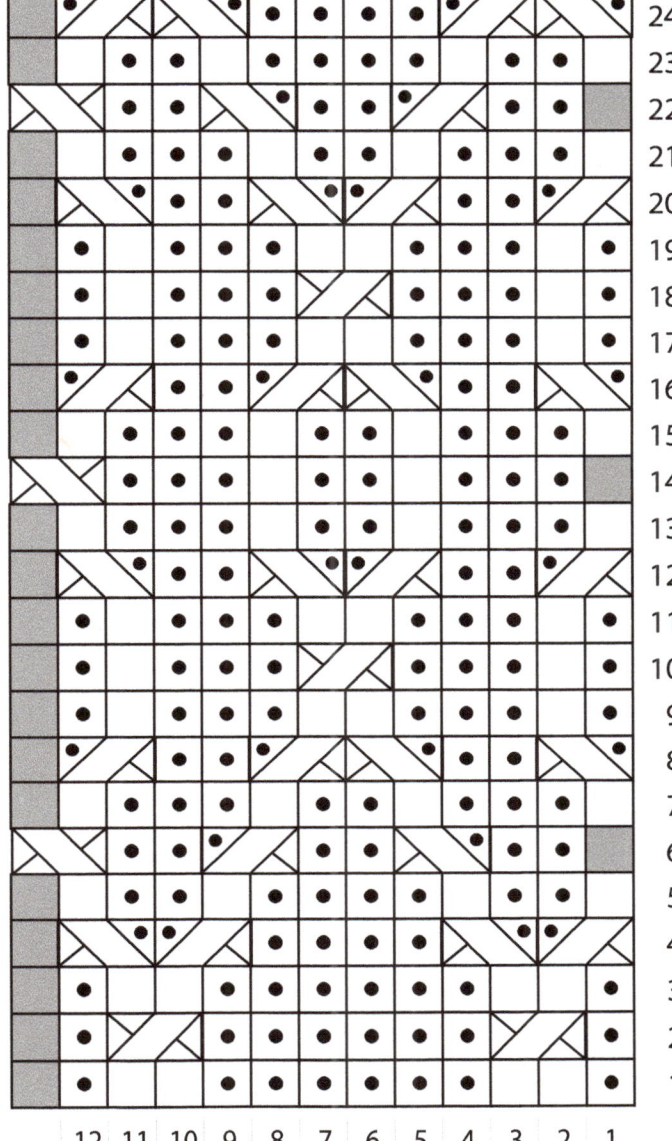

	Symbol	Meaning
	▨	No stitch
	□	Knit
	•	Purl
	⧄	1/1 RT
	⧅	1/1 LT
	⧄•	1/1 RTp
	⧅•	1/1 LTp

33

Josie

Josie is a mysterious character. Or is she?

Trophy wife? Hard edged business woman? However you view her, she definitely adds intrigue to the show. This cowl is intriguing, too. The color shifts happen automatically, so you can just concentrate on your knitting. Change up the colors to suit your many moods (and character traits).

Josie

MATERIALS

Cherry Tree Hill Broad Band Yarn [80% Superwash Merino/20% Mulberry Silk; 371 yds / 339.24m per 3.5 oz / 100g skein]; color: Cabin Fever

1 32" US#4 / 3.5mm circular needle

Large-eyed, blunt needle for weaving in ends

Stitch marker

MEASUREMENTS

Circumference:
27" (before blocking)
26" (after blocking)

Height:
9" (before and after blocking)

GAUGE

24 sts x 32 rnds = 4" square in stitch pattern A before blocking

STITCH PATTERN A

Rnd 1: K1, yo, ssk, k3, k2tog, yo; repeat to end of rnd

Rnd 2 (and all even rounds): Knit

Rnd 3: K2, yo, ssk, k1, k2tog, yo, k1; repeat to end of rnd

Rnd 5: K1, yo, ssk, yo, sl1, k2tog, psso, yo, k2tog, yo; repeat to end of rnd

Rnd 7: K2, yo, ssk, k1, k2tog, yo, k1; repeat to end of rnd

Rnd 9: K3, yo, sl1, k2tog, psso, yo, k2; repeat to end of rnd

Rnd 10: Knitneedle

STITCH PATTERN B

Rnd 1: K1, k2tog, k1, [yo, k1] twice, ssk; repeat to end of rnd

Rnd 2 (and all even rounds): Knit

Rnd 3: As rnd 1

Rnd 5: As rnd 1

Rnd 7: K1, yo, ssk, yo, sl1, k2tog, psso, yo, k2tog, yo; repeat to end of rnd

Rnd 9: K2, yo, ssk, k1, k2tog, yo, k1; repeat to end of rnd

Rnd 11: K3, yo, sl1, k2tog, psso, yo, k2; repeat to end of rnd

Rnd 12: Knit

FINISHING INSTRUCTIONS

Cast on 160 sts, and join to work in the round, placing a stitch marker to denote the beginning of the round.

Working repeats from either Chart A, or Stitch pattern A, for a total of 30 rounds (3 full repeats), then 3 full repeats from either Chart B or Stitch pattern B, for a total of 36 rnds, and then 3 more repeats from Chart A or Stitch pattern A (30 rounds)

Bind off loosely.

Wet block, pinning the points of each lace repeat for extra definition.

Josie

- ☐ Knit
- ○ Yarn over
- ◺ Ssk
- ◿ K2tog
- ⋀ Sl1, k2tog, psso

Chart A

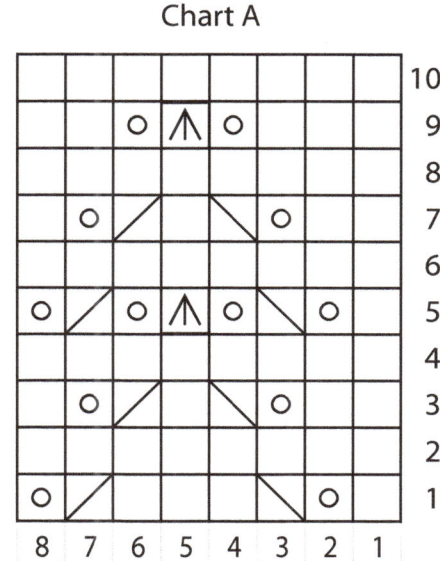

Chart B

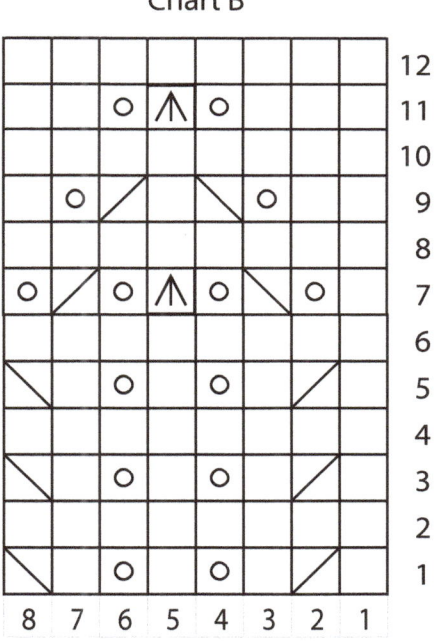

Laura

Laura Palmer is the one character even non-Twin Peaks fans know. Judging from the reaction to this cowl at the shows, you'll get the same amount of attention wearing it.

I am in love with Fiber Optic's Paintbox kits. I admit it: I've had one sitting on my kitchen island for the past two months just because I like looking at it and can't bear to put it away.

Laura

MATERIALS

Fiber Optic Blackbird Paintbox Gradient on Footnotes Yarn, 15 mini-skeins of 30 yds each [80% Superwash merino, 20% nylon, 450 yds / 411.48m total per 4.25 oz / 120g skein bundle]

1 32" US#4 / 3.5mm circular needle

Large-eyed, blunt needle, for weaving in ends

Stitch marker

MEASUREMENTS

Circumference:
23" (before blocking)
25" (after blocking)

Height:
8.5" (before blocking)
9" (after blocking)

GAUGE

28 sts and 36 rnds = 4" square in stitch pattern before blocking

STITCH PATTERN

Rnd 1: Knit

Rnds 2 - 4: Sl 3 wyib, k3; repeat to end of rnd

Rnds 5 - 7: Knit

Rnd 8: K1, gather stitch, k4; repeat to end of rnd

Rnd 9: Knit

Rnds 10 - 12: K3, sl 3 wyib; repeat to end of rnd

Rnds 13 - 15: Knit

Rnd 16: K4, *gather stitch, k1; repeat to end of rnd

GATHER STITCH

Insert RH needle under three strands on inside of cowl from bottom to top and place as sts on RH needle, p1 (on LH needle), pass 3 sts (on RH needle) over first st by inserting LH needle from left to right through these three sts ON THE INSIDE OF THE COWL.

FINISHING INSTRUCTIONS

With first mini-skein, loosely cast on 174 sts, join in the round, being careful not to twist, adding a stitch marker for beginning of rnd.

Work [k3, p3] ribbing for 7 rnds.

Switch to the next mini-skein

Work rnds 1 - 16 of the stitch pattern.

Switch to the next mini-skein.

Repeat this process until the last mini-skein.

Work [k3, p3] ribbing for 7 rnds, then bind off using Jeny's SSBO.

Weave in all ends, and block.

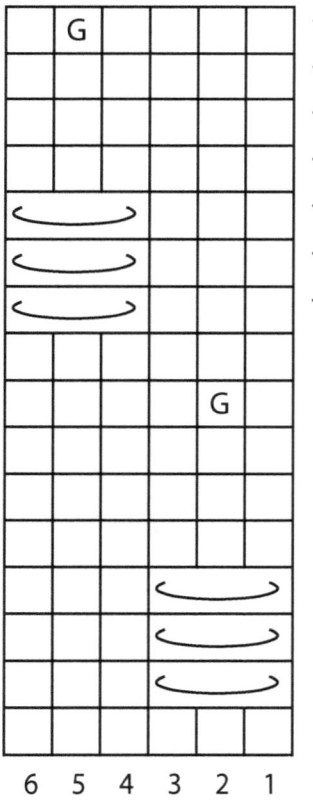

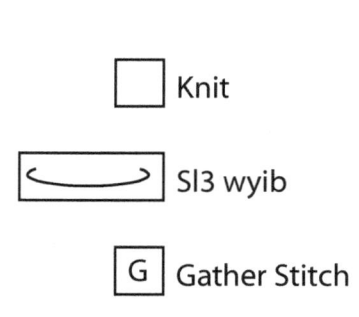

- ☐ Knit
- ⌒ Sl3 wyib
- G Gather Stitch

Nadine

Nadine's a character from Twin Peaks that cracks me up every time and also makes me sad.

You won't be sad knitting this yarn from Miss Babs, though: the chunky yarn flies off your needles and the colors, like all Miss Babs colors, are divine.

Nadine

MATERIALS

Miss Babs Hand Dyed Yarn & Fiber Kaweah Babette [100% superwash Merino wool, 280 yds / 255m per 4 oz / 113g skein]; color: Soul Food;

1 32" US#11 / 8mm circular needle

Large-eyed, blunt needle for weaving in ends

Cable needle (optional)

Stitch marker

MEASUREMENTS

Circumference:
28" (before blocking)
32" (after blocking)

Height:
10" (before blocking)
10" (after blocking)

GAUGE

12 sts x 16 rnds = 4" square in stitch pattern, before blocking

STITCHES USED

1/1 LT - slip 1 st to cable needle, hold in front, k1, k1 from cable needle

1/1 RT - slip 1 to cable needle, hold in back, k1, k1 from cable needle

1/1 LTp - slip 1 to cable needle, hold in front, p1, k1 from cable needle

1/1 RTp - slip 1 to cable needle, hold in back, k1, p1 from cable needle

STITCH PATTERN

Rnds 1 - 4: K1, p2, k1; repeat to end of rnd

Rnd 5: 1/1 LTp, 1/1 RTp; repeat to end of rnd

Rnd 6: P1, k2, p1; repeat to end of rnd

Rnd 7: P1, 1/1 RT, p1; repeat to end of rnd

Rnd 8: As rnd 6

Rnd 9: 1/1 RTp, 1/1 LTp; repeat to end of rnd

Rnds 10 - 14: As rnd 1

FINISHING INSTRUCTIONS

Cast on 100 sts, join to work in the round, adding a stitch marker to denote the beginning of the rnd.

Work [k1, p2, k1] rib for 12 rnds, then work repeats of the stitch pattern, or follow the chart until the cowl measures about 8.5" tall.

Work 12 rnds of rib, and bind off.

Lucy

Lucy the receptionist is sugary and sweet but don't make the mistake of underestimating her.

Ditto this cowl. The stitch pattern is challenging but well worth it. It also looks good on both sides, in my opinion.

Lucy

MATERIALS

Neighborhood Fiber Co Studio DK [100% Merino; 275 yds / 251m per 4 oz / 114g skein]; color: Victorian Village

1 32" US#5 / 3.75mm circular

US#6 / 4mm for cast on/bind off.

Large-eyed, blunt needle for weaving in ends

Stitch marker

MEASUREMENTS

Circumference:
22" (before blocking)
26" (after blocking cowl bottom flares to 30")

Height:
9" (before blocking)
9" (after blocking)

GAUGE

23 sts x 32 rnds = 4" square in stitch pattern before blocking

STITCH PATTERN

Rnd 1: P2, [k1tbl] twice, p3, p3tog, p3, [k1tbl] twice, p2, yo, k1tbl, yo; repeat to end of rnd.

Rnd 2: P2, [k1tbl] twice, p7, [k1tbl] twice, p2, k1, k1tbl, k1; repeat to end of rnd.

Rnd 3: P2 [k1tbl] twice, p2, p3tog, p2, [k1tbl] twice, p2, [k1tbl, yo] twice: repeat to end of rnd.

Rnd 4: P2, [k1tbl] twice, p5, [k1tbl] twice, p2, [k1tbl, k1] twice, k1tbl; repeat to end of rnd.

Rnd 5: P2, [k1tbl] twice, p1, p3tog, p1, [k1tbl] twice, p2, [k1tbl] twice, [yo, k1tbl] twice, k1tbl; repeat to end of rnd.

Rnd 6: P2, [k1tbl] twice, p3, [k1tbl] twice, p2, [k1tbl] twice, [k1, k1tbl] twice, [k1tbl] twice; repeat to end of rnd.

Rnd 7: P2, [k1tbl] twice, p3tog, [k1tbl] twice, p2, [k1tbl] twice, p1, yo, k1tbl, yo, p1, [k1tbl] twice; repeat to end of rnd.

Rnd 8: P2, [k1tbl] twice, p1, [k1tbl] twice, p2, [k1tbl] twice, p1, k1, k1tbl, k1, p1, [k1tbl] twice; repeat to end of rnd.

Rnd 9: P2, k1tbl, p3tog-tbl, k1tbl, p2, [k1tbl] twice, p2, yo, k1tbl, yo, p2, [k1tbl] twice; repeat to end of rnd.

Rnd 10: P2, [k1tbl] 3 times, p2, [k1tbl] twice, p2, k1, k1tbl, k1, p2, [k1tbl] twice; repeat to end of rnd.

Rnd 11: P2, p3tog-tbl, p2, [k1tbl] twice, p3, yo, k1tbl, yo, p3, [k1tbl] twice; repeat to end of rnd.

Rnd 12: P2, k1tbl, p2, [k1tbl] twice, p3, k1, k1tbl, k1, p3, [k1tbl] twice; repeat to end of rnd.

Rnd 13: P2, yo, k1tbl, yo, p2, [k1tbl] twice, p3, p3tog, p3, [k1tbl] twice; repeat to end of rnd.

Rnd 14: P2, k1, k1tbl, k1, kp2, [k1tbl] twice, p7, [k1tbl] twice; repeat to end of rnd.

Rnd 15: P2, [k1tbl, yo] twice, k1tbl, p2, [k1tbl] twice, p2, k3tog, p2, [k1tbl] twice; repeat to end of rnd.

Rnd 16: P2, [k1tbl, k1] twice, k1tbl, p2, [k1tbl] twice, p2, [k1tbl] twice, p5, [k1tbl] twice; repeat to end of rnd.

Rnd 17: P2, [k1tbl] twice, [yo, k1tbl] twice, k1tbl, p2, [k1tbl] twice, p1, p3tog, p1, [k1tbl] twice; repeat to end of rnd.

Rnd 18: P2, [k1tbl] twice, [k1, k1tbl] twice, k1tbl, p2, [k1tbl] twice, p3, [k1tbl] twice; repeat to end of rnd.

Rnd 19: P2, [k1tbl] twice, p1, yo, k1tbl, yo, p1, [k1tbl] twice, p2, [k1tbl] twice, p3tog, [k1tbl] twice; repeat to end of rnd.

Rnd 20: P2, [k1tbl] twice, p1, k1, k1tbl, k1, p1, [k1tbl] twice, p2, [k1tbl] twice, p1, [k1tbl] twice; repeat to end of rnd.

Rnd 21: P2, [k1tbl] twice, p2, yo, k1tbl, yo, p2, [k1tbl] twice, p2, k1tbl, p3tog-tbl, k1tbl; repeat to end of rnd.

Rnd 22: P2, [k1tbl] twice, p2, k1, k1tbl, k1, p2, [k1tbl] twice, p2, [k1tbl] 3 times; repeat to end of rnd.

Rnd 23: P2, [k1tbl] twice, p3, yo, k1tbl, yo, p3, [k1tbl] twice, p2, p3tog-tbl; repeat to end of rnd.

Rnd 24: P2, [k1tbl] twice, p3, k1, k1tbl, k1, p3, [k1tbl] twice, p2, k1tbl; repeat to end of rnd.

FINISHING INSTRUCTIONS

With larger needle, cast on 126 sts, join to work in the round, adding a stitch marker to show the beginning of the round.

Change to smaller needle - work repeats of the chart, or stitch pattern until you have about a third of the yarn left, and have completed either rnd 12 or rnd 24.

Work increase rnd 1 or 13 as set in the chart above the main chart, then work sts as they appear for 3 rnds.

With larger needle, bind off loosely.

Weave in ends and block.

Lucy

- ▨ No stitch
- ☐ Knit
- • Purl
- ○ Yarn Over
- ⃝ Ktbl
- P3tog
- K3tog tbl

Norma

Winter Woods is a favorite colorway of mine. So versatile!

If you like quieter colors, and simpler stitch patterns, this is the one for you. It's also chunky so it knits up quickly, which is great for last minute gifts.

Norma

MATERIALS

Dragonfly Fibers Super Traveller [100% superwash merino, 107 yards / 97.84m per 4 oz / 113g skein]; color: Winter Woods

1 32" US#11 / 8mm circular needle

Large-eyed, blunt needle for weaving in ends

Stitch marker

MEASUREMENTS

Circumference:
31" (before blocking)
27" (after blocking)

Height:
5½" (before blocking)
7½" (after blocking)

GAUGE

12 sts x 20 rnds = 4" square in stitch pattern before blocking

STITCH PATTERN

Rnd 1: P1, k3; repeat to end of rnd

Rnd 2: P1, yo, sl 1 kwise, k2tog, psso, yo; repeat to end of rnd

Rnds 3-10: Repeat rnds 1-2 four more times.

Rnd 11: Repeat rnd 1 once more.

FINISHING INSTRUCTIONS

Cast on 88 sts, and join to work in the round, being careful not to twist, and placing a stitch marker to denote beginning of rnd.

Work repeats of the stitch pattern or follow the chart until the cowl measures about 5.5" tall.

BO all sts as follows: K2, * sl 2 back to LH needle, k2tog tbl, k1; rep from * until 1 st remains. Break yarn, and thread through final stitch.

Weave in ends and block to finished measurements.

Important Note:
This cowl changes dimensions dramatically upon blocking. Please be sure to wet block, pinning the cowl to the after blocking measurements.

- ☐ Knit
- ◻ Purl
- ○ Yarn over
- ⋀ Sl1, k2tog, psso

Maddie

Carl and Eileen from Bijou Basin Ranch are also on my list of all-time favorites, both personally and for promoting yak fiber the way they do.

Soft, warm, beautiful. This lacy cowl goes with just about anything and the color looks good on almost everyone.

Maddie

MATERIALS

Bijou Basin Ranch Himalayan Trail, Yak/Merino Blend [75% Tibetan Yak / 25% Merino; 200 yd / 182.88m per 2 oz / 56g skein]; color: St. Andrews

1 32" US#5 / 3.75mm circular needle

1 US#6 / 4mm circular needle for cast on and bind off.

Large-eyed, blunt needle for weaving in ends

Stitch marker

MEASUREMENTS

Circumference:
25" (before blocking)
25" (after blocking)

Height:
9" (before blocking)
9" (after blocking)

GAUGE

23 sts = 4" in stitch pattern

STITCH PATTERN

Rnds 1, 3, 5, 7, 9, and 11: [Yo, k2tog] 4 times, k8; repeat to end of round

Rnds 2, 4, 8, 10, 13, 15, 19, and 21: Knit

Rnd 6: K8, 4/4 RC; repeat to end of rnd

Rnds 12, 14, 16, 18, 20, and 22: K8, [yo, k2tog] 4 times; repeat to end of rnd

Rnd 17: 4/4 RC, k8; repeat to end of rnd

FINISHING INSTRUCTIONS

With larger needle, cast on 144 sts, join to work in the round, adding a stitch marker to denote start of round.

Change to smaller needle - work repeats of the chart or stitch pattern until the cowl measures 9" tall.

Bind off with larger needle.

Wet block.

Maddie

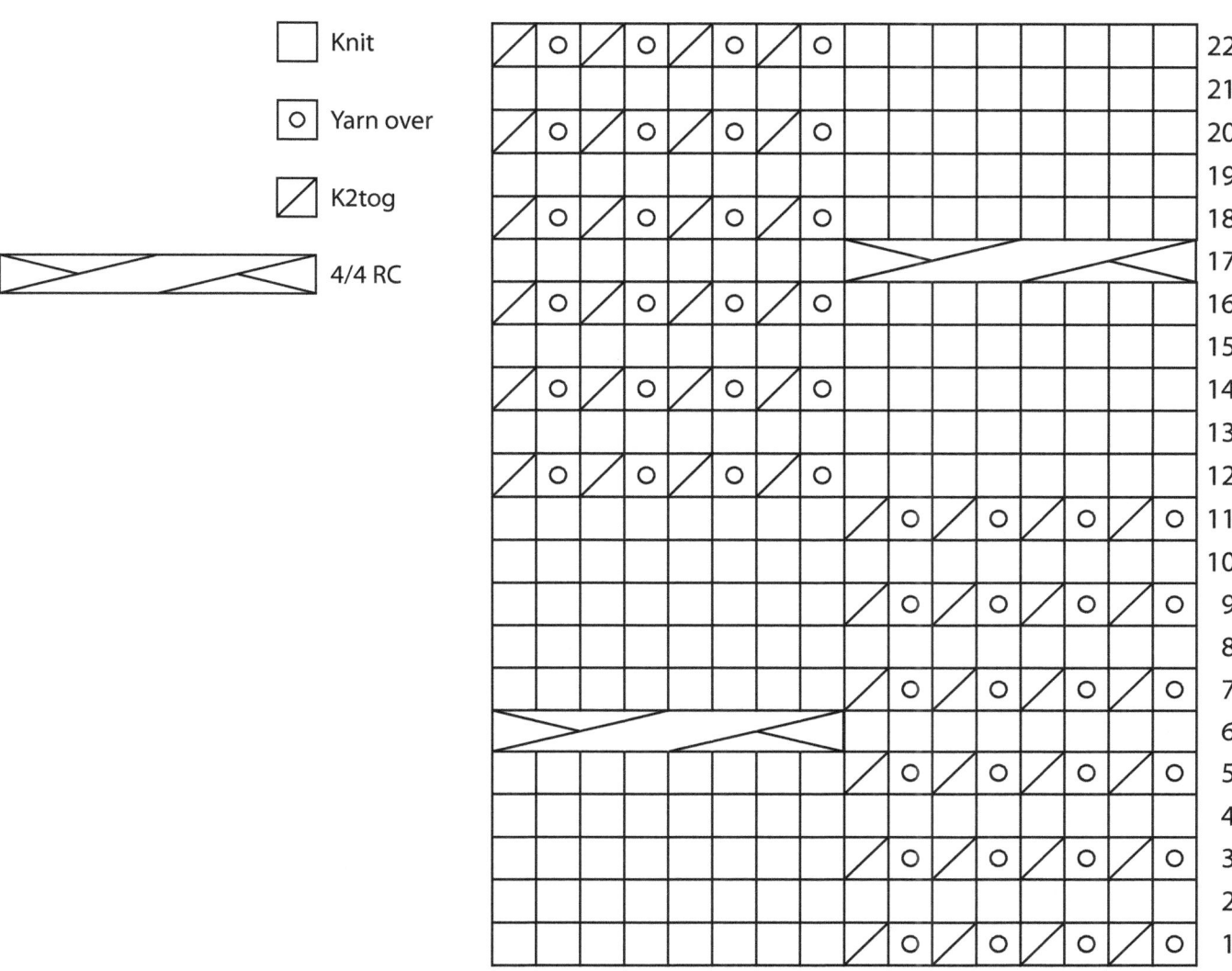

Ronette

Lisa, the Tsock Tsarina, created complex and amazing sock kits (usually with multiple colors) but this yarn, which was made for a specific project, HAD to be mine. The color was too, too perfect.

The stitch pattern, drawn from a Russian stitch dictionary, takes a little getting used to but is well worth it in the end.

Ronette

MATERIALS

Tsock Tsarina Tsilk Tsocking [70% Wool, 30% Silk; 400 yds / 366m per 3.53 oz / 100g skein]; color: Love a Hyacinth - DISCONTINUED

(A good high twist, alternate silk blend yarn is Marigold Jen's Merino Silk Sock [50% Wool Merino, 50% Silk; 438 yds / 401 m per 3.53 oz / 100g skein])

1 32" US#4 / 3.5mm circular needle

Large-eyed, blunt needle for weaving in ends

Stitch marker

MEASUREMENTS

Circumference:
22" (before and after blocking)

Height:
9" (before blocking)
9.5" (after blocking)

GAUGE

12 sts x 20 rnds = 4" in stitch pattern before blocking

EDGING PATTERN

Rnd 1: [P1, yo, k2tog]

Rnd 2: [P1, k2]

Rnd 3: [P1, ssk, yo]

Rnd 4: [P1, k2]

STITCH PATTERN

Rnd 1: *K1, yo, ssk, k7, k2tog, yo; repeat from * to end of rnd.

Rnd 2: *K1, yo, k1, ssk, k5, k2tog, k1, yo; repeat from * to end of rnd.

Rnd 3: *K1, yo, k2, ssk, k3, k2tog, k2, yo; repeat from * to end of rnd.

Rnd 4: *K1, yo, k3, ssk, k1, k2tog, k3, yo; repeat from * to end of rnd.

Rnd 5: *K1, yo, k4, sl1, k2tog, psso, k4, yo; repeat from * to end of rnd.

Rnd 6: *K4, k2tog, yo, k1, yo, ssk, k3; repeat from * to end of rnd.

Rnd 7: *K3, k2tog, k1, yo, k1, yo, k1, ssk, k2; repeat from * to end of rnd.

Rnd 8: *K2, k2tog, k2, yo, k1, yo, k2, ssk, k1; repeat from * to end of rnd.

Rnd 9: K1, k2tog, k3, yo, k`, yo, k3, ssk; repeat from * to end of rnd.

Rnd 10: Slip last st of previous rnd to beginning of this round, *sl1, k2tog, psso, k4, yo, k1, yo, k4; repeat from * to end of rnd.

FINISHING INSTRUCTIONS

Cast on 168 sts, and, being careful not to twist, join to work in the round.

Work 12 rnds of edging pattern (3 repeats).

Following either from the Ronette stitch pattern above, or from the chart, work repeats of the stitch pattern until cowl is 9 inches tall (or your desired height.

Work a further 12 rnds of edging pattern.

Bind off in pattern.

Weave in ends and block to measurements above.

Ronette

- □ Knit
- ○ Yarn over
- ◣ Ssk
- ◥ K2tog
- ∧ Sl1, k2tog, psso

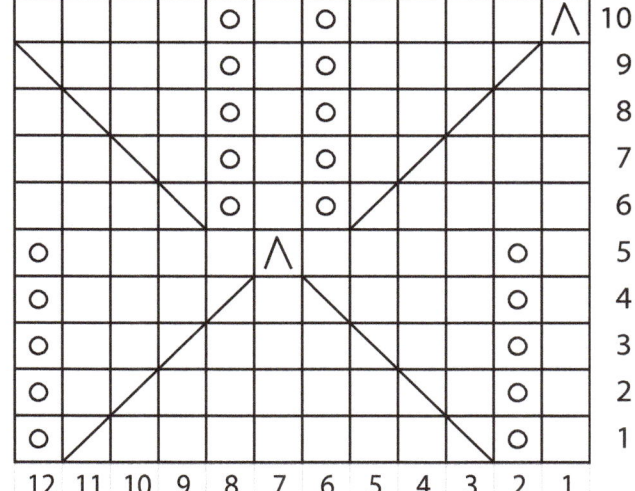

Shelly

We don't wear enough orange, if you ask me. It's such a happy color! I defy you to be sad wearing this.

Another lacy bit of goodness, this cowl. Simple and elegant, and adaptable to multiple yarn weights with ease if you want to go a bit thicker.

Shelly

MATERIALS

Marigoldjen Hand Dyed Sock Yarn [80% merino, 10% cashmere, 10% nylon; 400 yds / 366m per 4 oz / 113g skein]; color: Tangerine Speedo

1 32" US#6 / 4mm circular needle

1 US#7 /4.5 mm for cast on/bind off

Large-eyed, blunt needle for weaving in ends

Stitch marker

MEASUREMENTS

Circumference:
27" (before and after blocking)

Height:
8.5" (before and after blocking)

GAUGE

26 sts x 26 rnds = 4" in stitch pattern before blocking

STITCH PATTERN

Rnd 1: CDD, k4, yo, k1, yo; repeat to end of rnd

Rnd 2 (and all even rnds): Knit

Rnd 3: CDD, k3, yo, k1, yo, k1; repeat to end of rnd

Rnd 5: CDD, k2, yo, k1, yo, k2; repeat to end of rnd

Rnd 7: CDD, [k1, yo] twice, k3; repeat to end of rnd

Rnd 9: CDD, yo, k1, yo, k4; repeat to end of rnd

Rnd 11: As rnd 7

Rnd 13: As rnd 5

Rnd 15: As rnd 3

Rnd 16: Knit

FINISHING INSTRUCTIONS

With larger needle, cast on 168 sts, and join to work in the round.

Work repeats of chart, or stitch pattern until cowl is about 8.5" high.

Bind off with larger needle.

Weave in ends and block.

Note that the last stitch of each even row repeat becoes part of the following round CDD.

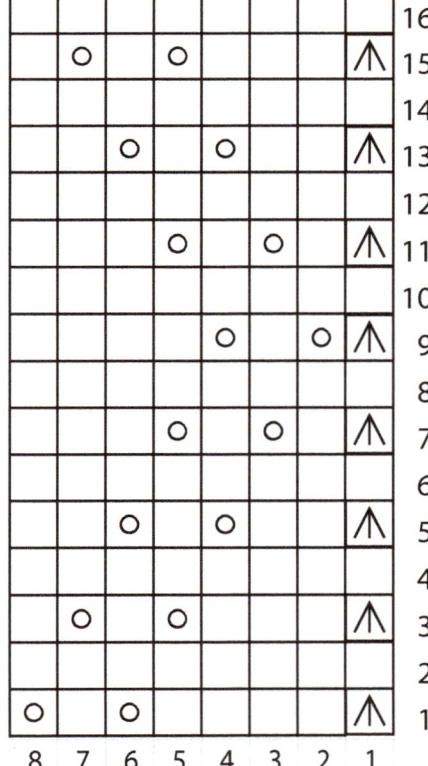

Abbreviations

approx.	approximate
beg	begin, beginning
bet	between
BO	bind off
CC	contrasting color
cm	centimeter
cn	cable needle
CO	cast on
cont	continue
dec	decrease or decreasing
dpn(s)	double-pointed needle(s)
est	established
foll	following
inc	increase or increasing
k	knit
k2tog	right-leaning decrease: knit 2 sts together as one
kfb	knit into front and back of a single stitch (increase)
LH	left-hand
m1	make one (increase)
MC	main color
p	purl
pm	place marker
rem	remain(s)/(ing)
rep	repeat
RH	right-hand
rnd	round
RS	right side (public side)
sl	slip
sm	slip marker
ssk	left-leaning decrease: sl 2 sts kwise one at a time, then knit them tog tbl
st(s)	stitch(es)
St st	stockinette stitch
tbl	through the back of the loop
tog	together
WS	wrong side (private side)
wyib	with yarn in back
wyif	with yarn in front
yd(s)	yard(s)
yo	yarn over

1/1 LT: Sl 1 to cn, hold in front. K1 tbl; k1 tbl from cn.

1/1 LTp: Sl 1 to cn, hold in front. P1; k1 tbl from cn.

1/1 RT: Sl 1 to cn and hold in back. K1 tbl; k1 tbl from cn.

1/1 RTp: Sl 1 to cn, hold in back. K1 tbl; p1 from cn.

Sl 3 wyib: Slip 3 sts with yarn at back of work

2/2 RC: Sl 2 to cn, hold in back. K2; k2 from cn.

2/2 LC: Sl 2 to cn, hold in front. K2; k2 from cn.

4/4 RC: Sl4 to cn, hold in back. K4; k4 from cn.

Chart Keys

▨	No stitch	⧖	K3tog tbl
☐	Knit	◬	k4tog
•	Purl	⋀	Sl 1, k2tog, psso
℞	Ktbl	⑦	Sl 4, k3tog, p4sso
○	Yarn over	G	Gather Stitch
V	K, p, k into st	◩	1/1 RT
╱	K2tog	◪	1/1 LT
╲	Ssk	◩•	1/1 RTp
⋏	Sl 1, k2tog, psso	•◪	1/1 LTp
⋏	Sl 1, k3tog, psso	⌣	Sl 3 wyib
⋀	Sl 2, k1, p2sso	⊠	2/2 RC
⋏₃	k3tog	⊠	2/2 LC
⋏₃	P3tog	⟨⊠⟩	4/4 RC

Basic Raglan

SIZES

Women's XS (S, M, L, XL, 2X, 3X); shown in size M

Intended to be worn with between 2 and 4 inches of positive ease, depending on the size.

MATERIALS

Approximately 1420 (1530, 1640, 1860, 2025, 2185, 2440) yards / 1300 (1400, 1500, 1700, 1850, 2000, 2230) m of fingering weight yarn

32 inch US# 2 / 2.75 mm circular needle

US# 2 / 2.75 mm needles configured for smaller circumference knitting - magic loop, dpns or two smaller circulars

4 removable stitch markers

Stitch holders or waste yarn

Yarn needle

FINISHED MEASUREMENTS

Bust: 34 (38, 42, 46, 50, 54, 58) inches.

GAUGE

32 sts and 40 rounds = 4 inches / 10 cm in stockinette stitch, on US# 2 / 2.75 mm needle

STITCHES AND TECHNIQUES

k - knit

m1 - make 1

p - purl

pm - place marker

rnd - round

sm - slip marker

PATTERN

Cast on on 118 (130, 144, 156, 168, 180, 194) sts. Being careful not to twist, join to work in the round.

Work 1 - 2 inches of rib of choice.

Rnd 1: K17 (19, 21, 23, 25, 27, 29) sleeve sts, pm, k40 (45, 49, 54, 58, 63, 67) front sts, pm, k17 (19, 21, 23, 25, 27, 29 sleeve sts, pm, k40 (45, 49, 54, 58, 63, 67) back sts, pm to denote end of round.

Rnd 2: Knit.

Rnd 3: Sm, [k1, m1, k to 1 st before next marker, m1, k1, sm] 4 times - 8 sts increased.

Rnd 4: Knit.

Repeat rnds 3 and 4 until there are 121 (134, 148, 161, 175, 188, 202) sleeve sts in each sleeve section, and 144 (160, 176, 192, 208, 224, 240) sts in each of the front/back sections.

Place first set of sleeve sts onto waste yarn or stitch holders.

Cast on 5 (5, 5, 6, 6, 7, 7) sts, work 144 (160, 176, 192, 208, 224, 240) sts in front section, cast on 5 (5, 5, 6, 6, 7, 7) sts, work 1 144 (160, 176, 192, 208, 224, 240) sts in back section - 298 (330, 362, 396, 428, 462, 494) sts total.

Work without shaping until body is 2 (2. 2.5, 2.5, 3, 3, 3) inches shorter than desired length. Work rib of your choice for remaining length.

Bind off in pattern.

Sleeves (both worked the same)

Pick up and knit 5 (5, 5, 6, 6, 7, 7) sts from underarm, then knit across 121 (134, 148, 161, 175, 188, 202) sleeve stitches, placing a marker at the end of the round - 126 (139, 153, 167, 181, 195, 209) total stitches. Working with either two circulars, long dpns, or the magic loop method, join to work in the round, and continue as follows:

Rnds 1 - 3: Knit.

Rnd 4: K1, ssk, k to last 3 sts, k2tog, k1.

Repeat rnds 1 - 4 until you have 52 (57, 63, 67, 75, 81, 86) sts.

Continue working without shaping, until sleeve is 2 (2. 2.5, 2.5, 3, 3, 3) inches shorter than desired length. Work rib of your choice for remaining length.

Bind off in patt. Weave in ends, graft gussets together. Block.

Pattern Name	Pattern repeat sts	Pattern repeat rounds
Audrey	12 sts	23 rnds
Diane Chart A	24 sts (this count changes)	47 rnds
Diane Chart B	12 sts	16 rnds
Log Lady	8 sts	12 rnds
Donna	18 sts	10 rnds
Grey-dient	18 sts	32 rnds
Harriet	12 sts	24 rnds
Josie Chart A	8 sts	10 rnds
Josie Chart B	8 sts	12 rnds
Laurie	6 sts	16 rnds
Nadine	4 sts	14 rnds
Lucy	18 sts	24 rnds
Maddie	16 sts	22 rnds
Ronette	12 sts	10 rnds
Shelley	8 sts	16 rnds